I Have Cuts and Scrapes

by Joanne Mattern

Content Consultant
Catherine A. Dennis, N.P.

Reading Consultant
Jeanne M. Clidas, Ph.D.
Reading Specialist

Children's Press®
An Imprint of Scholastic Inc.

Library of Congress Cataloging-in-Publication Data
Mattern, Joanne, 1963- author.
I have cuts and scrapes/by Joanne Mattern.
    pages cm. — (Rookie read about health)
Summary: "Introduces the reader to cuts and scrapes." — Provided by publisher.
Includes index.
ISBN 978-0-531-22705-3 (library binding) — ISBN 978-0-531-22581-3 (pbk.)
    1. Wounds and injuries—Juvenile literature. 2. First aid in illness and injury—
Juvenile literature. I. Title. II. Series: Rookie read-about health.
RD93.M38 2016
    617.1—dc23   2015021124

Produced by Spooky Cheetah Press
Design by Keith Plechaty

© 2016 by Scholastic Inc.

Photographs ©: cover: Laurent Chantegros/Getty Images; 3 top left: Hubskaya
Volha/Shutterstock, Inc.; 3 top right: jennyt/Shutterstock, Inc.; 3 bottom: hxdbzxy/
Shutterstock, Inc.; 4: 2xSamara.com/Shutterstock, Inc.; 7: Ann Cutting/Getty Images;
8: altrendo images/Media Bakery; 11: Image Source/Superstock, Inc.; 16: Carmen
MartA-nez BanAs/Getty Images; 19: martinedoucet/Getty Images; 20: Ariel Skelley/
Corbis Images; 23: Chuck Schmidt/Getty Images; 24: Clover No.7 Photography/
Getty Images; 27: Benjamin A. Peterson/Getty Images; 28: Ann Cutting/Getty
Images; 29 top left: Jon Schulte/Getty Images; 29 top right: wckiw/Shutterstock,
Inc.; 29 bottom: Chuck Schmidt/Getty Images; 30: Illustrated London News/Mary
Evans/The Image Works; 31 top: jallfree/iStockphoto; 31 center bottom: Carmen
MartA-nez BanAs/Getty Images; 31 bottom: Science Picture Co/Science Source.

Illustrations by Jeffrey Chandler/Art Gecko Studios!

Table of Contents

That Hurts!

Ouch! Maybe you touched
something sharp and cut
your finger. Perhaps you fell while
skating and scraped your knee.
Now you are bleeding!
You have a cut or a scrape.

This girl hurt her knee
when she fell. She was not
wearing knee pads.

Cuts and scrapes can really hurt. They can be scary, too. But they are usually nothing to worry about! Everyone gets a cut or a scrape sometimes.

What Is a Cut or a Scrape?

If you touch something sharp, you might cut yourself. A cut is an opening in your skin.

A scrape is different from a cut. Scrapes happen when something rubs away part of your skin.

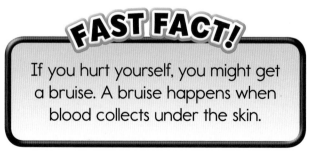

FAST FACT!

If you hurt yourself, you might get a bruise. A bruise happens when blood collects under the skin.

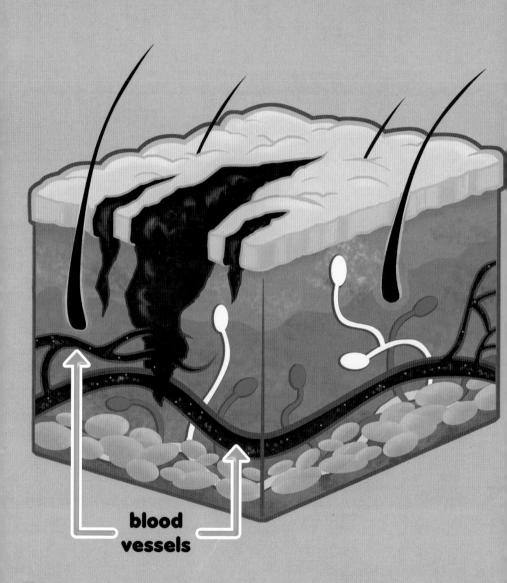

blood
vessels

After you get a cut or a scrape, you start bleeding. That is because you have torn tiny blood **vessels** under your skin.

This illustration shows what happens when you cut your skin.

Your body sends sticky cells called **platelets** to the cut. The platelets stick together to make a clot. A clot is like a plug that stops the bleeding.

Tiny platelets are joining together to form a clot.

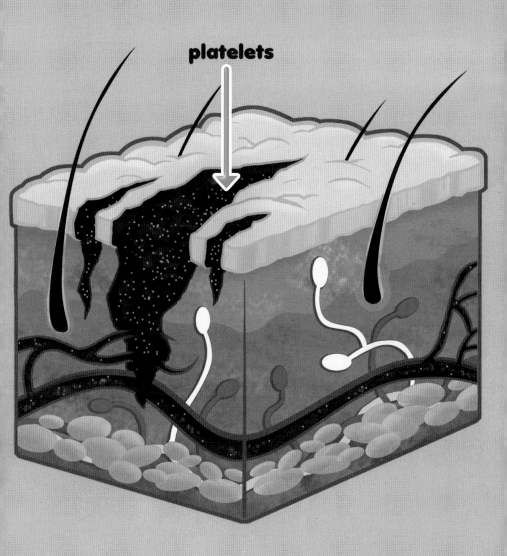

platelets

Soon a **scab** forms over the cut. It protects your skin. New skin grows underneath. When the cut is healed, the scab will fall off. Never pick at a scab! If you do, the cut will take longer to heal.

FAST FACT!

After a cut heals, you might have a scar. Most scars go away after a while. If the cut was deep, the scar might last forever.

Treating Your Wound

If you get a cut or a scrape, first try to stop the bleeding. Press a clean cloth on the cut. The bleeding should stop in a few minutes. If it does not, you might need to see a doctor.

FAST FACT!

If you have a cut on your hand, raise it so that it is above your heart. That will help it stop bleeding.

Next you should clean the cut.
Wash it with soap and water
to remove any dirt.

Put **antibacterial** medicine on the cut. Then cover it with a bandage. That will keep the cut clean.

FAST FACT!

Sometimes cuts get infected.
That means germs have gotten inside.
The wound may be swollen and red.
If this happens, tell an adult!

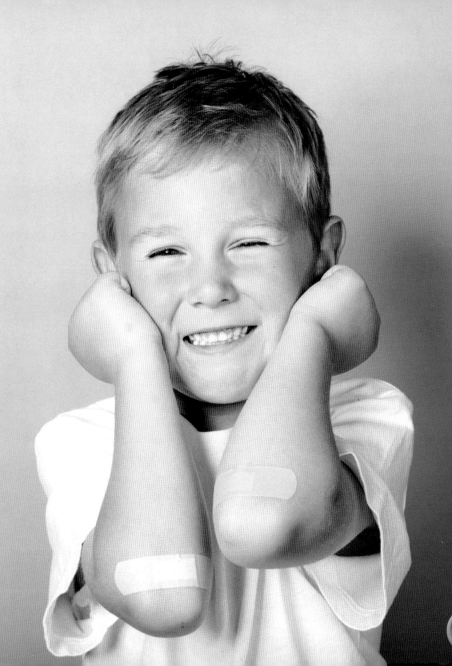

All Better!

It is hard to avoid cuts and scrapes completely. But you can protect yourself. Always be careful around sharp objects, like scissors. Wear knee pads when you skate. Safety gear will protect you if you fall.

Even if you do get a cut
or a scrape, do not worry.
Before long, your skin
will be healed!

Your Turn

Take this quiz to show what you know about cuts, scrapes, and your skin.

1. When you cut yourself, you tear blood vessels under your skin.
True or False?

2. Your body makes special cells to stop bleeding.
True or False?

3. It is not important to keep a cut or a scrape clean.
True or False?

Answers: 1. true; 2. true; 3. false

Healthy Healing

Look at the photos below. Which one shows something you should NOT do when you have a cut or a scrape?

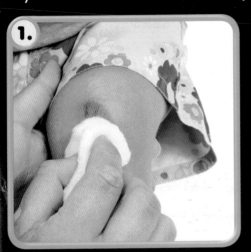

1.

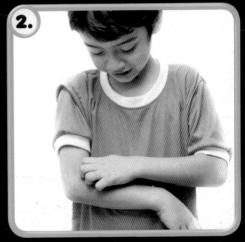

2.

3.

Answer: 2. You should never pick at a scab.

Strange but True!

In the past, doctors let cuts keep bleeding. They thought bleeding would clean out the wound.

Later, people used sticky spiderwebs to stop bleeding! During World War I, there was not enough cloth to make bandages when soldiers got hurt. So doctors made bandages out of moss instead.

Just for Fun

Q: What is a vampire's favorite game?

A: Follow the bleeder!

Q: What does a ghost get when he falls and scrapes his knee?

A: A boo boo!

Glossary

antibacterial (AN-tigh-bak-TEER-eh-uhl): able to kill germs

platelets (PLAYT-lits): tiny, sticky cells in the blood that help it clot

scab (skab): hard covering that forms over a wound when it is healing

vessels (VESS-uhls): tubes in the body that fluid (such as blood) passes through

Index

Facts for Now

Visit this Scholastic Web site for more information on cuts and scrapes:
www.factsfornow.scholastic.com
Enter the keywords **Cuts and Scrapes**

About the Author

Joanne Mattern is the author of many nonfiction books for children. She got many cuts and scrapes as she was growing up! She lives in New York State with her husband, four children, and numerous pets.